Animal Answers

Move to the head of the class with animal facts to help you pass!

by Carrie Anton

★ American Girl®

Published by American Girl Publishing
Copyright © 2013 by American Girl

Questions or comments? Call 1-800-845-0005, visit **americangirl.com**, or write to
Customer Service, American Girl, 8400 Fairway Place, Middleton, WI 53562-0497.

Printed in China
13 14 15 16 17 18 19 20 LEO 10 9 8 7 6 5 4 3 2 1

Editorial Development: Carrie Anton
Art Direction and Design: Sarah Boecher
Production: Kendra Schluter, Tami Kepler, Judith Lary
Illustrations: Thu Thai at Arcana Studios

INNERSTARU.com

Dear Reader,

Welcome to Innerstar University! At this imaginary, one-of-a-kind school, you can live with your friends in a dorm called Brightstar House and find lots of fun ways to develop new skills and let your true talents shine.

Follow your animal-loving guide, Amber, as she takes you on a journey to learn more about all kinds of mammals, reptiles, amphibians, birds, and fish. Using your animal-kingdom knowledge and Amber's tips, see if you can solve all the exciting mazes, riddles, and puzzles and complete the activities inside this book.

If you get stuck or just want to check your answers, turn to page 72. Have a good time finding your way through all the puzzles! Then head over to www.innerstarU.com for even more fun and games.

Your friends at American Girl

Innerstar Guides

Every girl needs a few good friends to help her find her way.

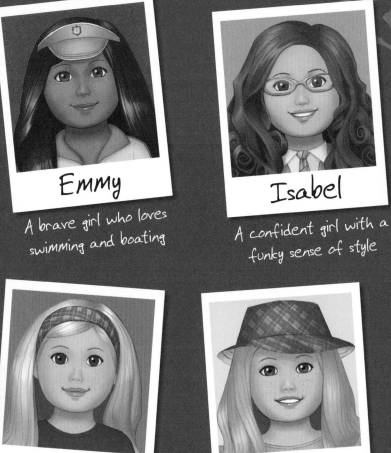

Emmy

A brave girl who loves swimming and boating

Isabel

A confident girl with a funky sense of style

Riley

A good sport, on the field and off

Paige

A nature lover who leads hikes and campus cleanups

Amber

An animal lover and a
loyal friend

Neely

A creative girl who loves
dance, music, and art

Logan

A super-smart girl
who is curious about
EVERYTHING

Shelby

A kind girl who is there
for her friends—and loves
making NEW friends!

Innerstar U Campus

1. Rising Star Stables
2. Star Student Center
3. Brightstar House
4. Starlight Library
5. Sparkle Studios
6. Blue Sky Nature Center

7. Real Spirit Center
8. Five-Points Plaza
9. Starfire Lake & Boathouse
10. U-Shine Hall
11. Good Sports Center
12. Shopping Square
13. The Market
14. Morningstar Meadow

Contents

Check it out, then check it off!

Answers start on page 72.

Meet Amber

Work side by side with your Innerstar University guide.

When it comes to animals, Innerstar University guide Amber is your go-to girl. Amber loves all creatures great and small—from rabbits to rhinos, eels to elephants, and hamsters to hyenas.

Because of Amber's fascination with furry, fishy, and feathered friends, she's the perfect guide to take you on an animal adventure. As you solve the critter puzzles throughout this book, Amber will share a few facts along the way. With Amber's eye for all things zoological and your own sharp animal instincts, you'll soon expand your knowledge of the creature kingdom.

Look for my speech bubbles for tips and guidance throughout the book.

INNERSTAR UNIVERSITY

Animal Jumble

Neely and Amber are painting a wild-animal mural together. Unscramble the words below to see which animals will be featured in their work of art. One or more letters of each animal name have been given to get you started.

1. gorilal
2. omgnoose
3. aolka
4. acgrou
5. oncabb
6. leopdar
7. adraakavr
8. jgraua
9. ecehath
10. aheyn
11. apnda
12. tgeir
13. rzeba
14. xof
15. erlum
16. peelnaht
17. horcerinso

1. g o r i l l a
2. m o n g o o s e
3. k o a l a
4. c _ _ _ _ _ _
5. b a b o o n
6. l e o p a r d
7. a a r d v a r k
8. j a g u a r
9. c h e e t a h
10. h y e n a
11. p a n d a
12. t i g e r
13. z e b r a
14. f o x
15. l e m u r
16. e l e p h a n t
17. r h i n o c e r o s

Animal Scene

In this outdoor scene, draw at least five of the animals whose names you unscrambled on page 11. Place the animals where they are most likely to hang out.

Baby Names

Just as young humans are called "babies," animals have unique baby names, too. Match the baby animal listed below with the type of animal it will grow up to be in the word search on the next page. To find the names, look up, down, backward, forward, and diagonally.

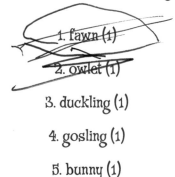

1. ~~fawn (1)~~
2. ~~owlet (1)~~
3. duckling (1)
4. gosling (1)
5. bunny (1)
6. lamb (1)
7. kitten (2)
8. ~~foal (3)~~
9. chick (4)
10. calf (4)
11. cub (5)

Different animals share the same baby names. For example, a dog, a wolf, and a hedgehog all start as pups. So the number next to each baby name means you are looking for that many different adult animals in the search. "Foal" is done for you.

INNERSTAR UNIVERSITY

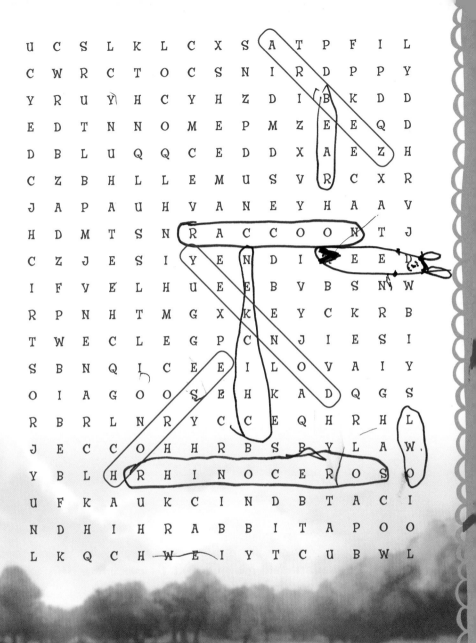

```
U  C  S  L  K  L  C  X  S  A  T  P  F  I  L
C  W  R  C  T  O  C  S  N  I  R  D  P  P  Y
Y  R  U  Y  H  C  Y  H  Z  D  I  B  K  D  D
E  D  T  N  N  O  M  E  P  M  Z  E  E  Q  D
D  B  L  U  Q  Q  C  E  D  D  X  A  E  Z  H
C  Z  B  H  L  L  E  M  U  S  V  R  C  X  R
J  A  P  A  U  H  V  A  N  E  Y  H  A  A  V
H  D  M  T  S  N  R  A  C  C  O  O  N  T  J
C  Z  J  E  S  I  Y  E  N  D  I  E  E  E  D
I  F  V  E  L  H  U  E  B  V  B  S  N  W
R  P  N  H  T  M  G  X  K  E  Y  C  K  R  B
T  W  E  C  L  E  G  P  C  N  J  I  E  S  I
S  B  N  Q  I  C  E  E  I  L  O  V  A  I  Y
O  I  A  G  O  O  S  E  H  K  A  D  Q  G  S
R  B  R  L  N  R  Y  C  C  E  Q  H  R  H  L
J  E  C  C  O  H  H  R  B  S  B  Y  L  A  W
Y  B  L  H  R  H  I  N  O  C  E  R  O  S  O
U  F  K  A  U  K  C  I  N  D  B  T  A  C  I
N  D  H  I  H  R  A  B  B  I  T  A  P  O  O
L  K  Q  C  H  W  E  I  Y  T  C  U  B  W  L
```

Puppy Picture

Guess the dog breeds below using the helpful hints. The letters circled in the answers show what colored circle stickers (provided in the back of the book) are needed to complete the picture.

This dog is a fast short-distance runner. (Hint: The first four letters tell you the color you get when you mix black and white.)

___ ___ ___ ___ ___ ___ ___ ___ ___

This short-haired terrier is said to be smart and full of energy. (Hint: Part of its name is also the capital of Massachusetts.)

_B_ _O_ _S_ _T_ _O_ _N_

This dog loves to play and has a lot of muscle. (Hint: It's also what a professional fighter who wears gloves is called.)

___ ___ ___ ___ ___

This short, flat-faced dog often has wrinkles and big eyes. (Hint: This dog's breed rhymes with "hug.")

___ ___ ___

This dog is typically white with black spots all over. (Hint: This breed is often linked with firefighters.)

___ ___ ___ ___ ___ ___ ___ ___ ___

This breed of dog sometimes has its hair groomed in a poufy style and comes in three sizes: standard, miniature, and toy. (Hint: In the 1950s, girls wore skirts that were named after this type of dog.)

___ ___ ___ ___ ___ ___

This wrinkled, muscular dog looks tough but typically has a sweet personality. (Hint: The first four letters spell the name of a male cow.)

___ ___ ___ ___ ___ ___ ___

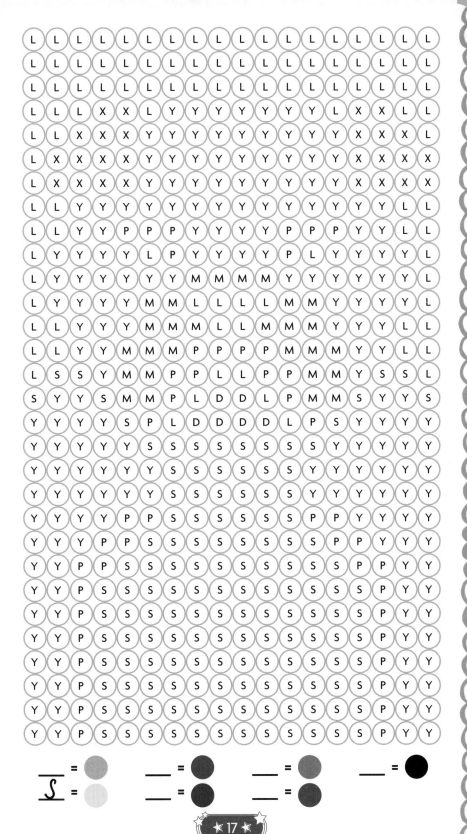

Pattern Problems

Oh no! Casual Closet received a batch of fun new animal T-shirts, but the designer got all of the animal prints confused. Complete the return sheet on the next page to help the designer correct the pattern problems.

I ♥ pandas!

I leap FOR LEOPARD

There's a spot in my heart for DALMATIANS!

Giraffe Girl

MOOVE IT!

BOAS are the BEST!

mean people
STINK!

Tigers are
terrific!

PARROTS ARE
PERFECT

Zebra
Crazy!

Return Sheet

Reason for return: *Animal patterns are wrong.*

How to fix: *Swap the patterns of the*

_____ and _____ , _____ and _____ ,

_____ and _____ , _____ and _____ ,

_____ and _____   *Thank you!*

Wild Designs

Now you get to be the designer! Create an animal-inspired T-shirt design that you think would sell well at Casual Closet. Use the small template tees below to sketch a few ideas. Then use the large shirt template on the right to draw a final design. One is done for you.

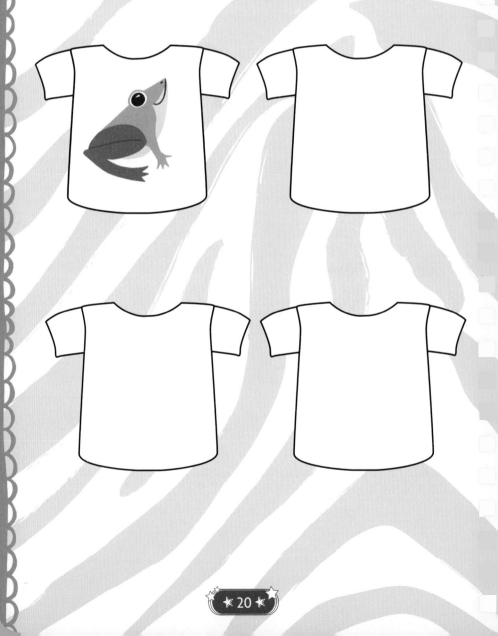

Critter Codes

Amber and Riley came up with this cool critter alphabet to send written messages in code. And you can use it, too! In this code, each critter's name begins with the letter of the alphabet it stands for. Use this code to read the riddles on pages 26 and 27.

A =

B =

C =

D =

E =

F =

G =

H =

I =

J =

K =

L =

M =

N =

O =

P =

Q =

R =

S =

T =

U =

V =

W =

X = Free

Y =

Z

Use the decoder from pages 22 and 23 to get the punch lines of these animal jokes.

1. What do you call a bear with no ears?

____ ! ____

2. What kind of dog loves to take baths?

____ ____ ____ ____ ____ ____ ____ ____ ____ ____

3. What do you get when you cross a porcupine with a balloon?

____ ____ ____ ! ____

4. What do you give to a pig with a rash?

____ ____ ____ ____ ____ ____ ____

5. What kind of can never needs a can opener?

____ ____ ____ ____ ____ ____ ____

6. What animal nevers tells the truth?

____ ____ ____ ____

7. How do fleas travel from place to place?

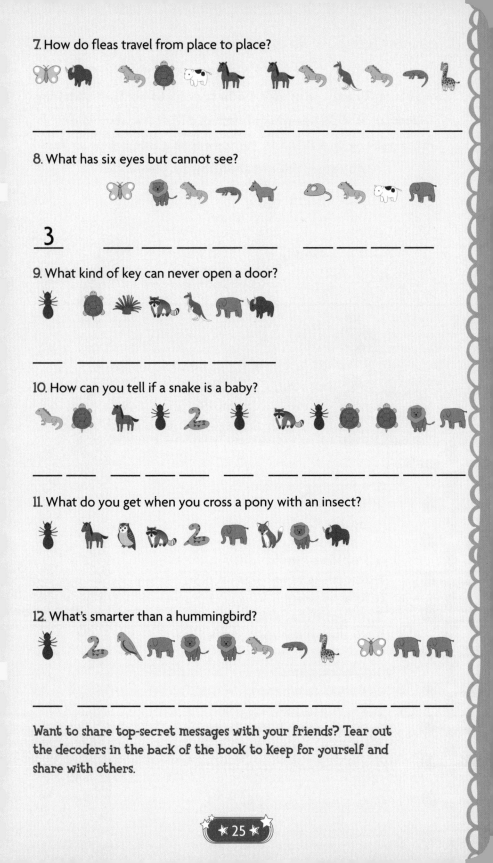

___ ___ ___ ___ ___ ___ ___ ___ ___ ___ ___

8. What has six eyes but cannot see?

3 ___ ___ ___ ___ ___ ___ ___ ___ ___

9. What kind of key can never open a door?

___ ___ ___ ___ ___ ___ ___ ___ ___

10. How can you tell if a snake is a baby?

___ ___ ___ ___ ___ ___ ___ ___ ___ ___ ___ ___ ___

11. What do you get when you cross a pony with an insect?

___ ___ ___ ___ ___ ___ ___ ___ ___ ___

12. What's smarter than a hummingbird?

___ ___ ___ ___ ___ ___ ___ ___ ___ ___ ___ ___ ___

Want to share top-secret messages with your friends? Tear out the decoders in the back of the book to keep for yourself and share with others.

Bird-Watching

Paige is really excited to add a new species to her bird-watching journal. To discover which feathered friend Amber found, cross out any bird that has the answer to a clue below as part of its name. The remaining bird is the answer.

finch

woodpecker

tanager

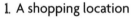
swallow

chickadee

1. A shopping location
2. What many soups come in at the grocery store
3. A place to hang a picture
4. Icky, slimey stuff
5. Something to wish upon at night
6. A fish's flapper
7. An animal that oinks
8. What meat does when it goes bad
9. To steal something
10. To talk extremely enthusiastically about
11. Add this to the end of "lemon" for a refreshing summer drink
12. What changes on your birthday
13. What you use oars for in a boat
14. A tool you use to pile up leaves

Amber's new feathered find

_____

A Frog's Life

The life cycle of a frog mainly consists of five stages. To help you understand each, Amber has created multiple mazes with a few froggy facts.

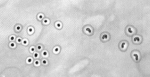

1. Egg: Frogs start in the water as eggs, which take an average of six to nine days to hatch.

2. Tadpole: Once an egg has hatched, the tadpole stage begins. At this time, the tadpole has fragile gills, a mouth, and a tail.

After seven to ten days, the tadpole begins to feed on algae and swim actively.

3. Tadpole with legs: At about six weeks old, the tadpole starts to form legs.

From six to nine weeks old, the tadpole begins to look like a tiny frog with a long tail.

When the froglet completes its full growth cycle after twelve to sixteen weeks, it leaves the water.

4. Froglet: After nine weeks the tadpole is considered a froglet because it looks like a small adult frog with just a stump of a tail.

5. Frog: Now full grown, the frog may return to the water to lay eggs and start a new life cycle.

Herd Huddle

Amber and Paige are volunteering on a local farm near Innerstar U. The farmer has asked the girls to group the cows by matching their cowhides. There are four groups. How many cows are in each?

A "cowhide" is another name for a cow's natural skin and hair.

INNERSTAR UNIVERSITY

Garden Guests

While planting flowers and vegetables in the garden at Blue Sky Nature Center, Paige comes across some unexpected guests. Can you find all 16 of them?

Home Sweet Home

Amber feels at home when she's hanging out with animal friends. Match the following animals with their correct habitats to help them all feel right at home.

1. tiger   2. seal   3. crocodile   4. camel   5. squid   6. bison

rain-forest

polar

wetland

desert

marine

grassland

Mammal Message

A hidden message is written in the connecting stripes and dots of the animals. Can you spot it?

Mammal message

_____

What's Eating You?

While hiking in the woods, Amber and Paige notice different parts of the food chain. There are *producers*—organisms such as plants that can create their own food. There are *consumers*—organisms such as animals that eat plants and other animals. And there are *decomposers*—oganisms such as bacteria and fungi that eat dead plants and turn them into nutrients for the soil. Group everything that Paige and Amber see. Draw a circle around the producers, a triangle around the consumers, and a square around the decomposers.

Class Crossword

All of the words below help to categorize animals into different groups called classes. Fit these animal-classification facts into the cross grid. One has been done for you. Then answer the question beneath the grid.

3 letters
fin
fur
web

4 letters
beak
head
horn

5 letters
claws
gills
hatch
lungs
wings

6 letters
scales

8 letters
antennae
backbone
feathers
flippers
omnivore
skeleton

9 letters
carnivore
herbivore

11 letters
cold-blooded
exoskeleton
warm-blooded

What class of animal is represented in the highlighted tiles?

_____

Camouflage Coloring

Amber and Neely are creating costumes for an upcoming play, for which animals in different scenes need to blend in with their backgrounds. Lend the guides a hand by coloring each animal's costume so that it is *camouflaged*, or disguised.

Ten animals are hanging out in the rain forest.
Can you find them all?

Tangled Tails

There is a mess of monkeys in the tree. Untangle their tails to see which one belongs to which monkey.

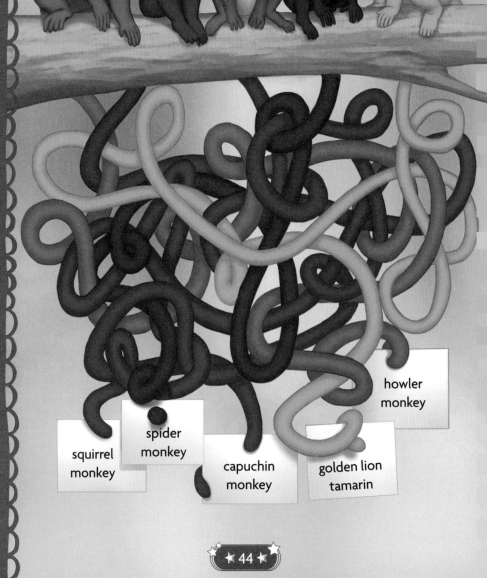

howler monkey

squirrel monkey

spider monkey

capuchin monkey

golden lion tamarin

Sea Search

While scuba diving on vacation, Amber saw all kinds of things in the ocean. Now you can find the same things in the word search below. To locate them, look up, down, backward, forward, and diagonally.

clam
coral
crab
kelp
manatee
plankton
saltwater
seashell
seaweed
shrimp
snail
starfish
stingray
turtle

```
S  P  C  O  R  A  L  Y  S  L
E  M  B  A  R  C  A  A  E  L
A  I  B  P  L  R  L  L  S  E
W  R  D  A  G  T  T  P  N  H
E  H  M  N  W  R  R  L  A  S
E  S  I  A  U  O  O  E  I  A
D  T  T  T  Z  W  T  K  L  E
S  E  H  S  I  F  R  A  T  S
R  P  L  A  N  K  T  O  N  T
E  E  T  A  N  A  M  J  H  E
```

Say What?

Learn about the following *idioms*—or familiar phrases—by writing in the correct animal to complete each saying. Each idiom has been defined for you. You can use each animal only once.

1. a _____ in a china shop (to be clumsy instead of careful)

2. A _____ in the hand is worth two in the bush. (What you have now is worth more than what you might get by taking a risk.)

3. quiet as a _____ (to make very little or no noise)

4. A _____ can't change its spots. (You are who you are and you can't change your basic character.)

5. Don't look a gift _____ in the mouth. (Don't be critical about a gift.)

6. Curiosity killed the _____. (Being too nosy can get you into trouble.)

7. _____ days of summer (very hot summer weather)

8. Don't count your _____s before they hatch. (Don't assume something before it happens.)

9. straw that broke the _____'s back (the small problem that causes everything to collapse)

10. _____ market (a sale of secondhand goods)

11. living high off the _____ (to live luxuriously)

12. to smell a _____ (to know that something is wrong or someone is lying to you)

13. 'til the _____ come home (until much later or the end of the day)

14. buy a _____ in a poke (get something without examining it first)

Canopy Critters

Hiding within the leaves, branches, and bark of the rain-forest trees are the names of species that typically live in the canopy. Find and write each one on the lines provided.

snake

ant

beetle

macaw

parrot

sloth

bat

hummingbird

tree frog

toucan

monkey

1. _____ 7. _____

2. _____ 8. _____

3. _____ 9. _____

4. _____ 10. _____

5. _____ 11. _____

6. _____

The rain forest is divided into four parts. At the highest is the emergent layer, under that is the canopy, below that is the understory layer, and the lowest level is the forest floor.

INNERSTAR UNIVERSITY

Hungry Herbivores

Amber needs to feed the hungry herbivores, but she doesn't know what there is to eat. Cross out the letters in "yum" to see who gets what for lunch.

1. y u m k
y u m y u m y u
m o y u m y u m y u
m y a u m y u l m y u
m y u m y u a m y u
m y u m y u m y
u m y u m

2. y u
m y u m
a y u m y
u n m y u
m y u m t
y u m y u
m y u m y
u m e y u
l m y u m
o y u m p
y u m y u
e m y u
m

3. y u s m y u m y u m y u m y u m y u m y u m y
u m y u h m y u m y u m y u m y u m y u m y u m y
u m y u m y u m y u m e y u m y u m e y u m y u m y
u m y u m y u m y u m y u m y u m
p y u m

An "herbivore" is an animal that feeds only on plants. Animals that feed only on meat are called "carnivores," whereas "omnivores" are animals that eat plants _and_ meat.

4. yumyugmy
umyumyumyum
yiumyumyumyum
yumyumyumryumy
uamyumyumyumy
umyufmyumfyu
meyumyumy

5. yumyumyum
yumyumyumyum
yumyurmyumyumyu
myumyhumyumyumyum
yumyumyumyumyiumyu
myumyumyumy
umyumnyumyu
myumyumoy
umyumyumy
umyum

6. yumyum
yubmyumyum
yumeyumyumyumyu
myumyumyumyaumyu
myumyumyumvyumey
umyumyumyrumyu
myumyumyu
myum

7. yumyru
myumyumyumy
umayumyumyumy
umyubmyumyumyub
myumyumyumyumy
umyumyuimyumyu
mtyumyumyumy
umyumyumy

8. yum
yumhyum
yumyumyuom
yumyumumyumy
umyumryumyumyu
myumyumyumyusm
yumyumyumyumyu
myumyumyumyu
myumyumyumy
umyumeyumy
umyumyum
yumyum
yum

While camping, Amber, Riley, and Logan hear noises outside their tent. Can you find all nine nocturnal animals that are hiding in the night?

Predator vs. Prey

Predatory animals feed on smaller, weaker animals called prey. Most animals are both predators and prey. Draw arrows below to indicate how the food chain works.

A Day at the Zoo

Amber and her friends each have a favorite attraction at the zoo. They're planning a Saturday visit and want to make sure to include everyone's favorites. Use the clues below to complete the grid and see how the girls fit in all the fun.

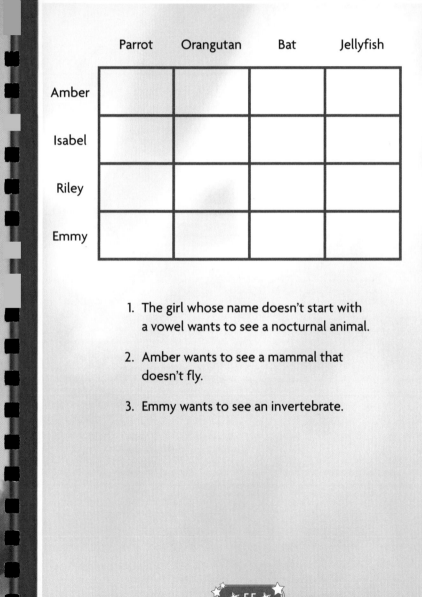

	Parrot	Orangutan	Bat	Jellyfish
Amber				
Isabel				
Riley				
Emmy				

1. The girl whose name doesn't start with a vowel wants to see a nocturnal animal.

2. Amber wants to see a mammal that doesn't fly.

3. Emmy wants to see an invertebrate.

Three's Company

Amber dropped a pile of animal flash cards while shuffling and came across an interesting discovery. When combining the names of two different animals, you can sometimes form a third animal's name. Pair up the flash cards on these two pages and write on the line the new animal it forms. Use each card only once.

fly

chicken

bull

tiger

seal

fish

turtle

horse

dog

hawk

deer

tick

spider

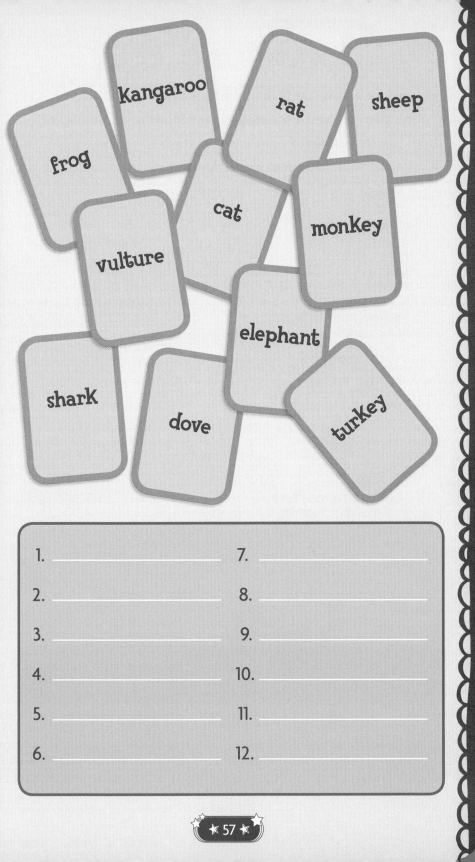

kangaroo

rat

sheep

frog

cat

monkey

vulture

elephant

shark

dove

turkey

1. _____
2. _____
3. _____
4. _____
5. _____
6. _____

7. _____
8. _____
9. _____
10. _____
11. _____
12. _____

Concealed Eels

Yikes! The eel exhibit tank at the Blue Sky Nature Center broke. Now all of the eels are hiding in the following words. Identify each "eel" word to help return them to a new tank. The first one is done for you.

1. a tumbling move

   C   A   R   T   W   H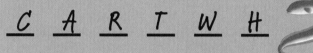

2. the back part of the foot

   _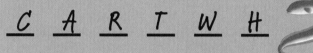

3. a physical sensation

   _ 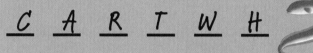 _   _   _

4. to rest on bended legs

   _   _

5. a round toy with colored spokes

_ _ _ _ _

6. a tool to remove potato skins

_ _ _ _

7. to unwind

_ _ _

8. to vote someone into office again

_ _ _ _ _

9. a straight line between two places

_ _ _ _ _

10. a hard metal

_ _

An eel is a bony fish that looks a lot like a slippery snake.

INNERSTAR UNIVERSITY

Name That Noise

Humans use the word "talk" to describe how they communicate, and they also have words to describe the sounds that animals make. See if you can unscramble the sound listed next to each animal below.

1. dolphin   lckic   _____

2. grasshopper   ripett   _____

3. dog   rbka   _____

4. duck   kcauq   _____

5. falcon   ntcah   _____

6. bear   wlrgo   _____

7. wolf   lohw   _____

8. rhinoceros   norst   _____

9. sheep   tleab   _____

10. chicken   cclake   _____

11. bird   nisg   _____

12. goose   okhn   _____

13. tortoise   ntugr   _____

14. owl   hoto   _____

15. sparrow   hircp   _____

16. snake   shsi   _____

17. pig   ueqlas   _____

18. hyena   ghalu   _____

19. turkey   bloebg   _____

20. horse   hegin   _____

21. frog   ckoar   _____

22. eagle   cerasm   _____

23. beetle   nerdo   _____

24. ape   bebgri   _____

25. donkey   arby   _____

26. parrot   aklt   _____

27. elephant   pttremu   _____

28. bee   bzzu   _____

29. lion   oarr   _____

30. fox   eply   _____

Pond Prowl

Amber sees 14 animals while walking around the pond.
Can you find everything she spotted?

Desert Dweller

Some alphabet letters are missing from the desert scene. Use the missing letters to find the animal that lives in this habitat.

Creature Celebration

Shelby and Paige went over the top setting up Amber's animal-themed surprise birthday party. With all of the decorations, how well do you remember the scene? Look at it carefully, and then turn the page and fill in the details.

Creature Celebration

**See how well you remember the animal-party scene
by answering these quick questions.**

1. What animal print is shown on the tablecloth?

   _____

2. What animal is sitting on top of the cake?

   _____

3. What shape are the wall decals?

   _____

4. Which animal face is shown on the blue balloon?

   _____

5. What type of stuffed animal is Amber holding?

   _____

6. How many different animals are shown on the two
   banners: 14, 16, 21, or 25?

   _____

7. What animal is shown on the purple party hat?

   _____

Spine Tingling

All of the animals listed below have something in common—they're all vertebrates. Unscramble each animal name to see what makes an animal a vertebrate.

1. cabbot
2. dota
3. leinapc
4. ksnea

5. nobboa
6. sinbo
7. natu
8. lee

1. __ __ __ __ __ __

2. __ __ __ __

3. __ __ __ __ __ __ __

4. __ __ __ __ __

5. __ __ __ __ __ __

6. __ __ __ __ __

7. __ __ __ __

8. __ __ __

An invertebrate is the opposite of a vertebrate.

Color-In Clues

Amber has left you an animal riddle. To solve her riddle, you must answer the questions below. The circled letter of each answer corresponds with a color. Color in the picture on the next page to reveal the hidden answer.

I always sleep with my shoes on. What am I?

Cold-blooded, vertebrate animals such as snakes, turtles, and lizards are called

● ___ ___ ___ ___ ___ ___ ___

An animal that has a hard outer structure such as a shell is said to have an

___ ___ ___ ___ ● ___ ___ ___ ___ ___

A robin typically lays her eggs in a

● ___ ___ ___

Shaped like something in the night sky, you can find this invertebrate underwater. What is it?

___ ___ ___ ___ ___ ___ ● ___

What animal has eight arms?

___ ___ ___ ___ ___ ___

What bird looks similar to a penguin but has webbed feet?

___ ___ ● ___ ___ ___

An animal that eats only meat is called a

● ___ ___ ___ ___ ___ ___ ___

An animal's home environment is also called a

___ ___ ___ ___ ● ___

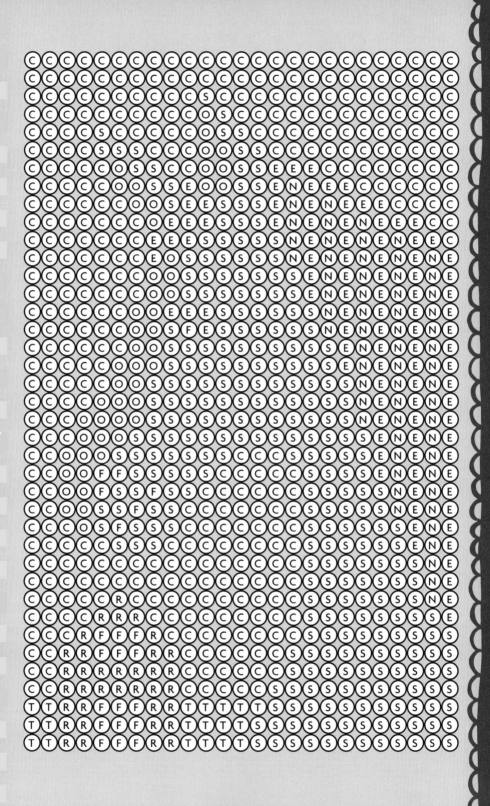

Snowy Search

There are nine arctic animals hiding in the snowy, cold polar region. Can you find them all?

Answers

Animal Jumble

Page 11

1. gorilla
2. mongoose
3. koala
4. cougar
5. baboon
6. leopard
7. aardvark
8. jaguar
9. cheetah
10. hyena
11. panda
12. tiger
13. zebra
14. fox
15. lemur
16. elephant
17. rhinoceros

Baby Names

Pages 14–15

1. deer
2. owl
3. duck
4. goose
5. rabbit
6. sheep
7. cat, beaver
8. horse, donkey, zebra
9. chicken, crane, emu, ostrich
10. cow, rhinoceros, camel, whale
11. cheetah, bear, hyena, lion, raccoon

Puppy Picture

Pages 16–17

1. greyhound (letter Y)
2. boston (letter S)
3. boxer (letter X)
4. pug (letter P)
5. dalmatian (letter M)
6. poodle (letter D)
7. bulldog (letter L)

Pattern Problems

Pages 18–19

panda and leopard
zebra and giraffe
cow and tiger
skunk and boa constrictor
parrot and dalmatian

Critter Codes

Pages 24–25

1. B!
2. a shampoodle
3. POP!
4. oinkment
5. a pelican
6. a lion
7. by itch hiking
8. 3 blind mice
9. a turkey
10. It has a rattle.
11. a horsefly
12. a spelling bee

Bird-Watching

Pages 26–27

1. **mall**ard
2. **can**ary
3. s**wall**ow
4. **goo**se
5. **star**ling
6. **fin**ch
7. **pig**eon
8. par**rot**
9. **rob**in
10. **rave**n
11. chick**adee**
12. tan**ager**
13. **crow**
14. pa**rake**et

Amber's new feathered friend: woodpecker

A Frog's Life

Pages 28–29

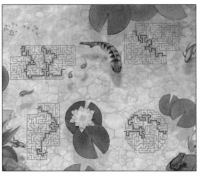

Herd Huddle

Pages 30–31

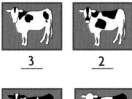

3   2

5   2

Garden Guests

Pages 32–33

Home Sweet Home

Page 34

1. tiger   rain-forest
2. seal   polar
3. crocodile   wetland
4. camel   desert
5. squid   marine
6. bison   grassland

Mammal Message
Page 35

UR AN ANIMAL 2
(You are an animal, too.)

What's Eating You
Pages 36–37

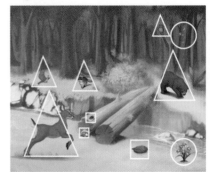

Class Crossword
Pages 38–39

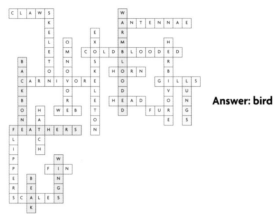

Answer: bird

Rain-Forest Find
Pages 42–43

Tangled Tails
Page 44

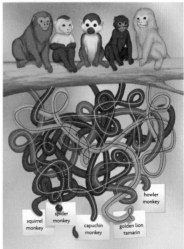

howler monkey

squirrel monkey

spider monkey

capuchin monkey

golden lion tamarin

Sea Search
Page 45

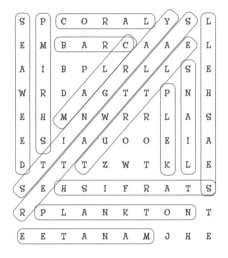

Say What?
Pages 46–47

1. bull
2. bird
3. mouse
4. leopard
5. horse
6. cat
7. dog
8. chicken
9. camel
10. flea
11. hog
12. rat
13. cows
14. pig

Canopy Critters
Pages 48–49

parrot
macaw
hummingbird
toucan
beetle
snake
monkey
sloth
bat
tree frog
ant

Hungry Herbivores
Pages 50–51

1. eucalyptus
2. lichens
3. grass
4. apricot
5. alfalfa
6. aspen leaves
7. lettuce
8. carrot
koala
antelope
sheep
giraffe
rhino
beaver
rabbit
horse

Night Crawlers
Pages 52–53

Predator vs. Prey
Page 54

A Day at the Zoo
Page 55

	Parrot	Orangutan	Bat	Jellyfish
Amber		X		
Isabel	X			
Riley			X	
Emmy				X

Three's Company
Pages 56–57

catfish
tiger shark
sheepdog
turkey vulture
spider monkey
deer tick
chicken hawk
horsefly
turtle dove
bullfrog
elephant seal
kangaroo rat

Concealed Eels
Pages 58–59

1. cartwhEEL
2. hEEL
3. fEELing
4. knEEL
5. pinwhEEL
6. pEELer
7. unrEEL
8. rEELect
9. bEELine
10. stEEL

Name That Noise
Pages 60–61

1. click	11. sing	21. croak
2. pitter	12. honk	22. scream
3. bark	13. grunt	23. drone
4. quack	14. hoot	24. gibber
5. chant	15. chirp	25. bray
6. growl	16. hiss	26. talk
7. howl	17. squeal	27. trumpet
8. snort	18. laugh	28. buzz
9. bleat	19. gobble	29. roar
10. cackle	20. neigh	30. yelp

Pond Prowl
Pages 62–63

Desert Dweller
Page 64
Answer: gecko

Creature Celebration
Pages 65–66
1. giraffe
2. hippopotamus
3. butterfly
4. cat
5. monkey
6. 16
7. zebra

Spine Tingling
Page 67
1. boBcat
2. toAd
3. peliCan
4. snaKe
5. baBoon
6. bisOn
7. tuNa
8. eEl
Answer: backbone

Color-In Clues
Pages 68–69
1. reptiles (letter r)
2. exoskeleton (letter e)
3. nest (letter n)
4. starfish (letter s)
5. octopus (letter u)
6. puffin (letter f)
7. carnivore (letter c)
8. habitat (letter t)

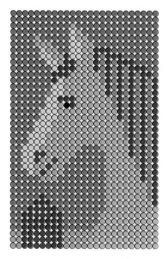

Snowy Search
Pages 70–71

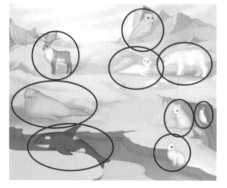

INNERSTARU.COM

The puzzle fun continues online!

Use the code below for access to
even more puzzles and activities.

Go online to innerstarU.com/puzzle
and enter this code: ANIMALFUN

Basic System Requirements:
Windows: Internet Explorer 7 or 8, Firefox 2.0+, Google Chrome
Mac: Safari 4.0+
Monitor Resolution: Optimized for 1024 x 768 or larger
Flash Version 10 and high-speed Internet required

Requirements may change. Visit www.innerstarU.com for
full requirements and latest updates.

Important Information:
Recommended for girls 8 and up. American Girl reserves the right
to modify, restrict access to, or discontinue www.innerstarU.com
at any time, in its sole discretion, without prior notice.

Here are some other American Girl books you might like:

❑ I read it.

❑ I read it.

❑ I read it.

❑ I read it.

❑ I read it.

❑ I read it.

Puppy Picture Stickers

Use these stickers to complete the picture on page 17.

Decoder

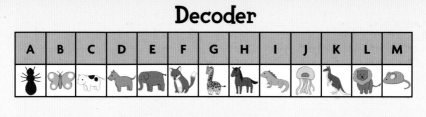

Decoder

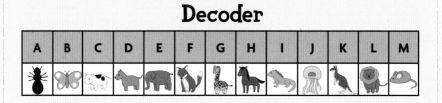

Decoder

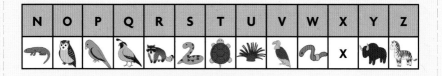

Decoder

N	O	P	Q	R	S	T	U	V	W	X	Y	Z

True or false? A *species* is a subgroup into which scientists classify just flying animals.

An *herbivore* is an animal that feeds only on _____.

True or false? A *cowhide* is another name for a cow's favorite sleeping spot.

Mammals are animals that are warm-blooded, have _____, and breathe with lungs.

Animals use _____ to help them hide from predators.

True or false? One layer of the rain forest is called the *canopy*.

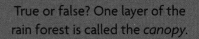

plants

False. A species is a subgroup into which scientists classify living things.

backbones

False. A cowhide is another name for a cow's hair and skin.

True. The rain forest is divided into four parts. At the highest is the emergent layer, under that is the canopy, below that is the understory layer, and the lowest level is the forest floor.

camouflage

Animals that feed only on meat are called_____.

An animal without a backbone is called an _____.

True or false? *Predators* are animals that feed only on seafood.

An eel is a bony _____ that looks a lot like a slippery snake.

Omnivores are animals that eat _____ and _____.

True or false? As a human, you are an example of a vertebrate.

invertebrate

carnivores

fish

False. Predators are animals that feed on other animals.

True. Humans have backbones, which makes them vertebrates

plants, animals